KAYA

and the Guardians of the Sacred Water

STORY MAGIC PRESS

"A young girl emerged from indian tribes, striving to revive the beauty that once flourished, amidst the filthy rivers and tarnished skies. She took on the role of the water's voice and the land's protector,

reminding us all of our responsibility to look for and restore our beloved planet and to protect the water and the land from pollution.

The sun rises on a peaceful land,
Where a young girl wakes and takes a stand.

In a beautiful land of streams and trees, Lived a girl who loved the river and the breeze.

A girl from a tribe, with a heart full of pride, Looked at the river and the land by her side.

She hears the river's gentle sound,
And sees the beauty all around.

She woke up one day, feeling so dismayed, The river was ruined, she was afraid.

She followed the river upstream,
And saw the factories, like a
nightmare dream.

She saw factories that rose so high,
Polluting the water and polluting the
sky.

She knew her tribe had the power and might,To protect the water and make everything right.

Kaya felt the river's call in her heart, And knew she had to act and do her part.

Kaya ran fast to the village square, To gather the tribe and make them aware.

She shouted, "Come one, come all,
We must go and answer the water's call!"

She gathers her tribe, and they make a plan, To heal the river, and protect their land.

They organize and form a plan,
To fight the factory and make a
stand.

They plant more trees, and clean up the trash, The river starts to heal, with a gentle splash.

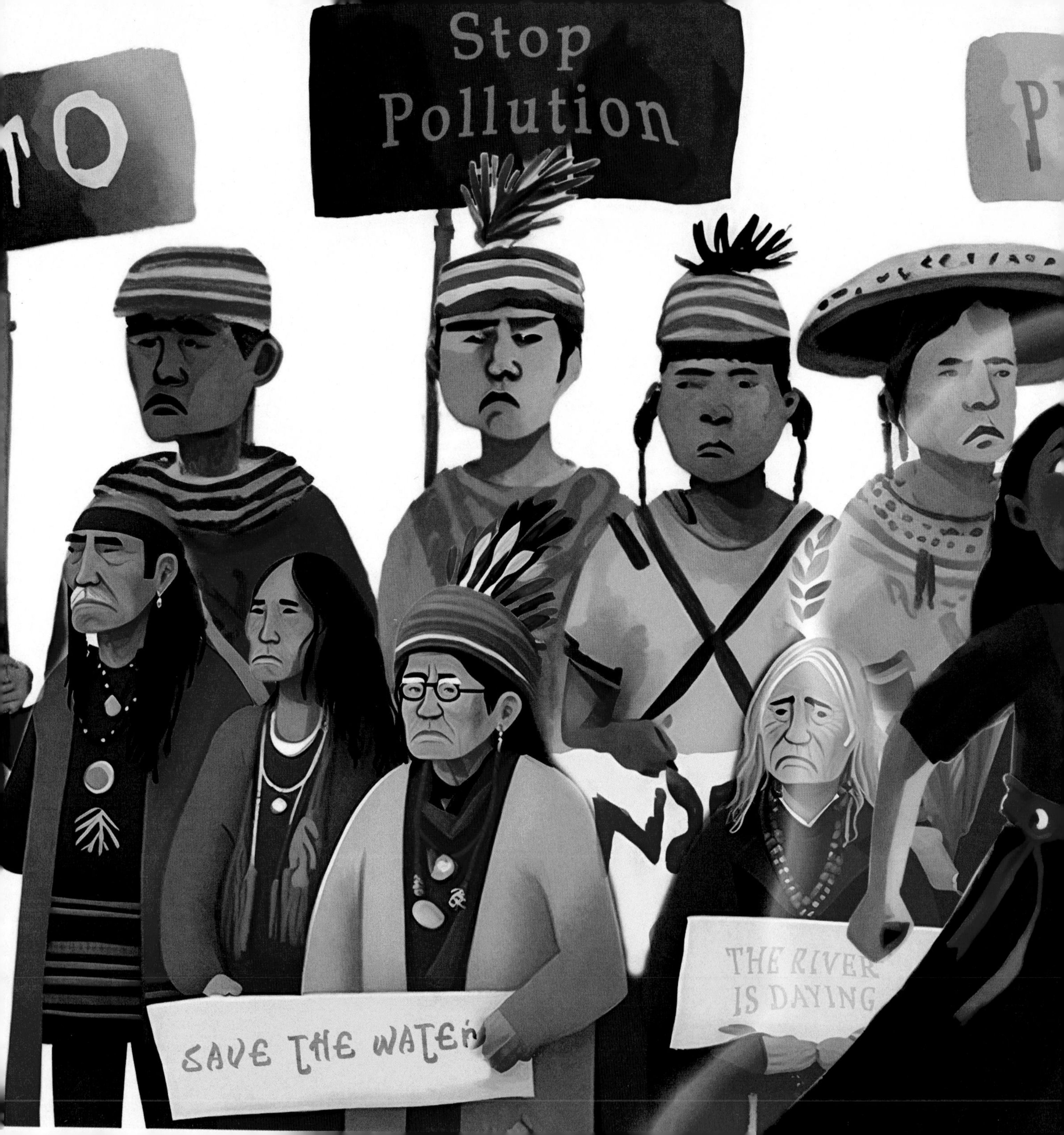
Stop
Pollution
SAVE THE WATER
THE RIVER
IS DAYING

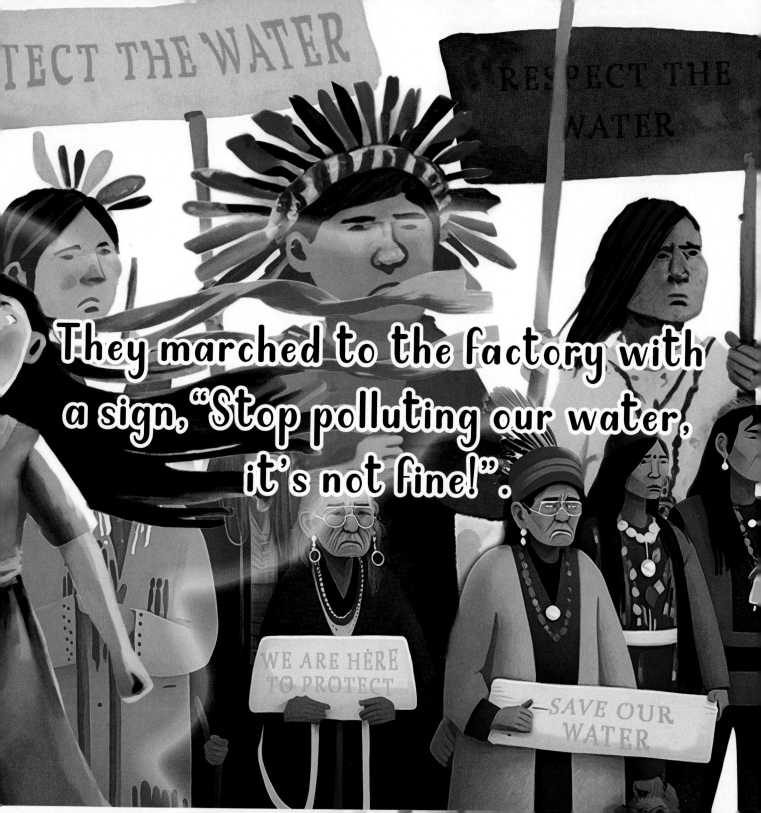

They marched to the factory with a sign, "Stop polluting our water, it's not fine!".

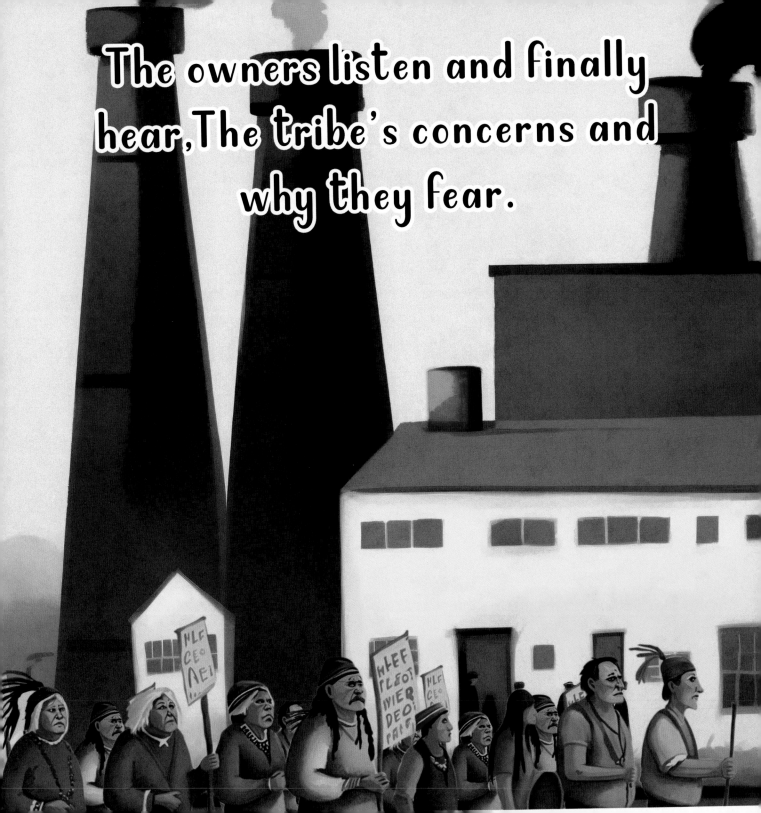

The owners listen and finally hear,The tribe's concerns and why they fear.

The factories pledged to make amends, and use green energy that never ends.

The water sparkles and flows so bright,The land is beautiful and full of light.

The river flowed freely, the land was so green, And the creatures came back, to this magical scene.

Now the water was pure, and the land was green, And the girl knew she had fulfilled her dream.

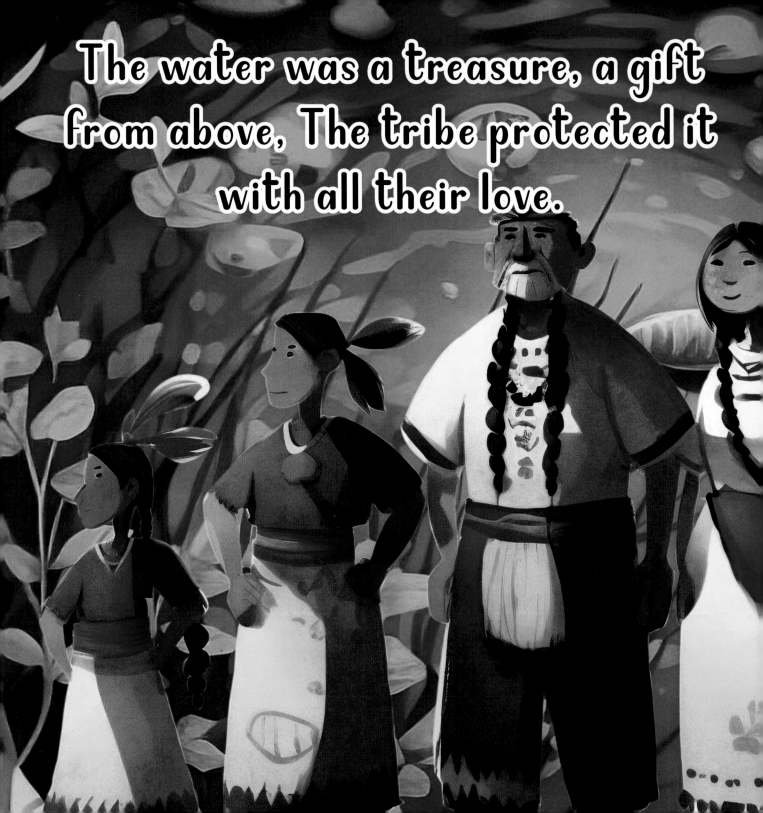

The water was a treasure, a gift from above, The tribe protected it with all their love.

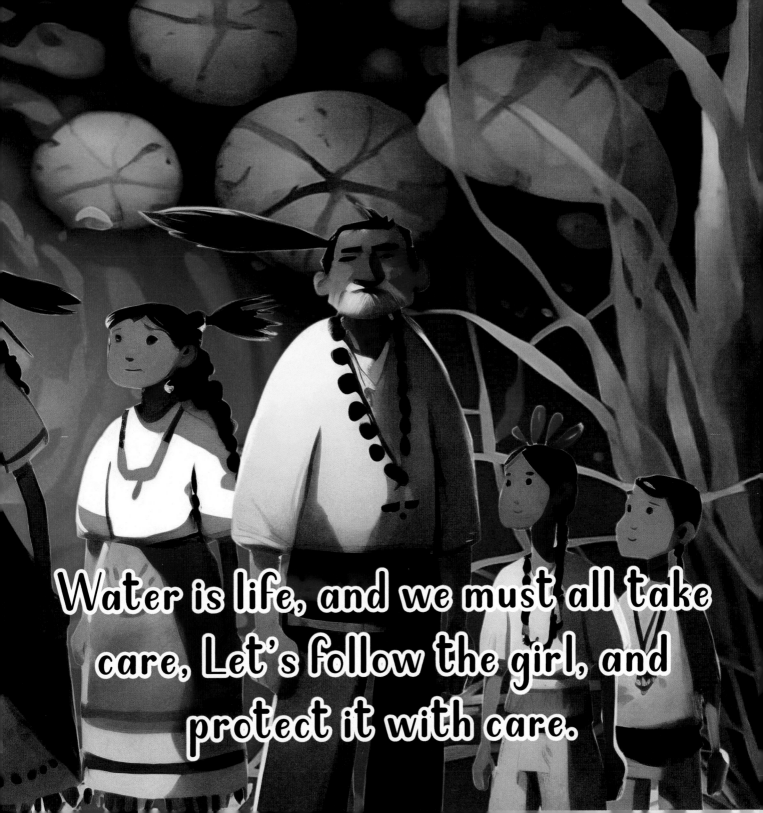

Water is life, and we must all take care, Let's follow the girl, and protect it with care.

Let's Explore the Wonders of Water!

-Water covers about 71% of the Earth's surface.

-The human body is about 60% water, and it is necessary for bodily functions like digestion, circulation, and temperature regulation.

-Water is used to generate electricity through hydropower.

-Water helps transport nutrients and oxygen throughout plants and animals.

-Water is essential for all living things to survive and grow.

Ways to Save Water

-Just by turning off the tap while you brush your teeth in the morning and before bedtime, you can save as much as 4 to 8 gallons of water! That could add up to more than 200 gallons a month, enough to fill a huge fish tank that holds 6 small sharks! The same is true when you wash dishes.

-Taking a shower uses much less water than filling up a bathtub. A shower only uses 10 to 25 gallons, while a bath takes up to 70 gallons! If you do take a bath, be sure to plug the drain right away and adjust the temperature as you fill the tub. To save even more water, keep your shower under five minutes long try timing yourself with a clock next time you hop in!

-Fixing a toilet leak is a great way to reduce household water use and boost water conservation. If your toilet leaks, you could be wasting about 200 gallons of water every day. That would be like flushing your toilet more than 50 times for no reason!

Ways to Prevent Pollution

-Planting trees! Trees help clean the air we breathe. So, we can plant trees in our yards or participate in tree-planting events to make our environment cleaner and healthier.

-We should turn off lights and electronics when we're not using them. And when it's time to go outside, we can walk, bike, or take the bus instead of using a car. This helps reduce air pollution and keeps our air clean."

Made in the USA
Las Vegas, NV
10 September 2023